Red Hen lived in a house next to a wood. In the wood lived a fox.

The fox longed to cook
Red Hen for dinner.

It was a chilly morning and Red Hen was out collecting sticks.

The fox had hidden in the trees, and was waiting for her.

As Red Hen collected
some sticks, the fox ran
out from the trees,...

...flung his sack around Red Hen, and quickly tied up the top.

Red Hen was trapped!

As she bumped along in the sack, Red Hen shouted out, "I will be a much better dinner if you add some carrots and garlic."

"Mmm! That sounds good,"
said the fox, licking his lips,
and ran off to get some.

Snip, snip, went Red Hen,
until there was room for her
to squeeze out of the sack.

She found a big rock, hid it in the sack, and mended the cut.

Then she ran quickly back to her house.

The fox had found some
carrots and garlic.

He ran back, grabbed
the sack and took it
to his house.

He started boiling a big pot,
chopped up the carrots and garlic,
and then tried to add Red Hen.

SPLASH!
The rock fell into the pot.

The fox was shocked and angry. He shouted, "I will get you, Red Hen, just you wait!"